THE CHINESE HOROSCOPES LIBRARY

MONKEY

KWOK MAN-HO

DORLING KINDERSLEY
LONDON • NEW YORK • STUTTGART

A DORLING KINDERSLEY BOOK

Senior Editor	Sharon Lucas
Art Editor	Camilla Fox
Managing Editor	Krystyna Mayer
Managing Art Editor	Derek Coombes
DTP Designer	Doug Miller
Production Controller	Antony Heller
US Editor	Laaren Brown

Artworks: Danuta Mayer 4, 8, 11, 17, 27, 29, 31, 33, 35;
Giuliano Fornari 21; Jane Thomson; Sarah Ponder.

Special Photography by Steve Gorton. Thank you to the Bristol City Museum & Art Gallery,
Oriental Section; The British Museum, Chinese Post Office, The Fan Museum – Hélène
Alexander Collection, The Powell-Cotton Museum, and The Board of Trustees of the
Victoria & Albert Museum.

Additional Photography: Eric Crichton, Jo Foord, Philip Gatward, Steve Gorton, Dave King,
Stephen Oliver, Tim Ridley, Matthew Ward.

Picture Credits: Circa Photo Library 12, The Fan Museum – Hélène Alexander Collection,
19cl, Courtesy of The Board of Trustees of the Victoria & Albert Museum 13.

First American Edition, 1994
2 4 6 8 10 9 7 5 3

Published in the United States by Dorling Kindersley Publishing, Inc., 95 Madison Avenue,
New York, New York 10016

Copyright © 1994
Dorling Kindersley Limited, London
Text copyright © 1994 ICOREC

ISBN 1-56458-604-9
Library of Congress Catalog Number 93-48006

Reproduced by GRB Editrice, Verona, Italy
Printed and bound in Hong Kong by Imago

CONTENTS

INTRODUCING CHINESE HOROSCOPES

For thousands of years, the Chinese have used their astrology and religion to establish a harmony between people and the world around them.

The exact origins of the twelve animals of Chinese astrology – the Rat, Ox, Tiger, Rabbit, Dragon, Snake, Horse, Ram, Monkey, Rooster, Dog, and Pig – remain a mystery. Nevertheless, these animals are important in Chinese astrology. They are much more than general signposts to the year and to the possible good or bad times ahead for us all. The twelve animals of Chinese astrology are considered to be a reflection of the Universe itself.

YIN AND YANG SYMBOL
White represents the female force of yin, and black represents the masculine force of yang.

every single thing in the Universe is held in balance by the dynamic, cosmic forces of yin and yang. Yin is feminine, watery, and cool; the force of the Moon and the rain. Yang is masculine, solid, and hot; the force of the Sun and the Earth. According to ancient Chinese belief, the concentrated essences of yin and yang became the four seasons, and the scattered essences of yin and yang became the myriad creatures that are found on Earth.

The twelve animals of Chinese astrology are all associated with either yin or yang. The forces of yin rise as Winter approaches. These forces decline with the warmth of Spring, when yang begins to assert

YIN AND YANG

The many differences in our natures, moods, health, and fortunes reflect the wider changes within the Universe. The Chinese believe that itself. Even in the course of a normal day, yin and yang are at work, constantly changing and balancing. These forces also naturally rise and fall within us all.

Everyone has their own internal balance of yin and yang. This affects our tempers, ambitions, and health. We also respond to the changes of weather, to the environment, and to the people who surround us.

THE FIVE ELEMENTS

All that we can touch, taste, or see is divided into five basic types or elements – wood, fire, earth, gold, and water. Everything in the Universe can be linked to one of these elements.

For example, the element gold is linked to the Monkey and to the Rooster. This element is also linked to the color white, acrid-tasting food, the season of Autumn, and the emotion of sorrow. The activity of these elements indicates the fortune that may befall us.

AN INDIVIDUAL DISCOVERY

Chinese astrology can help you balance your yin and yang. It can also tell you which element you are, and the colors, tastes, parts of the body, or emotions that are linked to your particular sign. Your fortune can be prophesied according to the year, month, day, and hour in which you were born. You can identify the type of people to whom you are attracted, and the career that will suit your character. You can understand your changes of mood, your reactions to other places and to other people. In essence, you can start to discover what makes you an individual.

DIVINATION STICKS
Another ancient and popular method of Chinese fortune-telling is using special divination sticks to obtain a specific reading from prediction books.

CASTING YOUR HOROSCOPE

The Chinese calendar is based on the movement of the Moon, unlike the calendar used in the Western world, which is based on the movement of the Sun.

Before you begin to cast your Chinese horoscope, check your year of birth on the chart on pages 44 to 45. Check particularly carefully if you were born in the early months of the year. The Chinese year does not usually begin until January or February, and you might belong to the previous Chinese year. For example, if you were born in 1961 you might assume that you were born in the Year of the Ox. However, if your birthday falls before February 15 you belong to the previous Chinese year, which is the Year of the Rat.

THE SIXTY-YEAR CYCLE

The Chinese measure the passing of time by cycles of sixty years. The twelve astrological animals appear five times during the sixty-year cycle, and they appear in a slightly different form every time. For example, if you were born in 1944

you are a Monkey Climbing a Tree, but if you were born in 1980, you are a Monkey in the Fruit Tree.

MONTHS, DAYS, AND HOURS

The twelve lunar months of the Chinese calendar do not correspond exactly with the twelve Western calendar months. This is because Chinese months are lunar, whereas Western months are solar. Chinese months are normally twenty-nine to thirty days long, and every three to four years an extra month is added to keep approximately in step with the Western year.

One Chinese hour is equal to two Western hours, and the twelve Chinese hours correspond to the twelve animal signs.

The year, month, day, and hour of birth are the keys to Chinese astrology. Once you know them, you can start to unlock your personal Chinese horoscope.

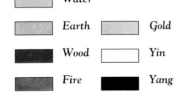

Water

Earth

Wood

Fire

Gold

Yin

Yang

CHINESE ASTROLOGICAL WHEEL

In the center of the wheel is the yin and yang symbol. It is surrounded by the Chinese astrological character linked to each animal. The band of color indicates your element, and the outer ring reveals whether you are yin or yang.

· MONKEY ·
MYTHS AND LEGENDS

The Jade Emperor, heaven's ruler, asked to see the Earth's twelve most interesting animals. When they arrived, he was impressed by the Monkey's mischievousness, and awarded it ninth place.

Monkeys appear in many Chinese legends. In South China, there are ancient stories of women being ravished by monkeys, and then giving birth to monkey-children. Several clans attribute their origin to the union of a woman and a monkey.

MONKEY AND FRIENDS
Monkey leads the line of legendary characters on this 17th-century wall carving from the Great Pagoda in Chengdu, China.

In this area of China, the monkey god is worshipped as the "Great Sage Equal to Heaven." However, in popular imagery he is also associated with adultery. Pictures of monkeys riding on horses were traditionally given as presents with the wish that the recipient may be promoted soon.

THE LEGEND OF MONKEY
Monkeys appear as gods in the Chinese novel *Journey to the West*, also

TWO JADE MONKEYS
These finely carved jade monkeys are holding a peach, a symbol of longevity. They are from China's Ch'ing dynasty (1750–1800).

known as *Monkey*. This is the most famous epic in China. Monkey, the king of the monkeys, caused great trouble on Earth, so the Jade Emperor invited him to heaven and gave him a heavenly post. But it was a very lowly post.

Enraged, Monkey departed for his beloved monkey army on earth. The Jade Emperor sent heavenly warriors after him, but Monkey defeated them all. Delighted, Monkey erected a banner inscribed "Great Sage Equal to Heaven."

The skills of Kuan Yin, the goddess of mercy, eventually captured Monkey, but Buddha was the deity who humbled him.

Monkey was brought before the Buddha. Gathering Monkey into his hand, the Buddha said, "I challenge you to jump out of my hand." Monkey laughed, and said, "I can jump to the universe's edge." "Go ahead," said the Buddha, "but leave your mark when you get there." So Monkey rushed through millions of miles, until he arrived at five giant pillars. Here, he wrote "The Great Sage Equal to Heaven was here" and urinated on the middle pillar. He returned to the Buddha's hand. "I have done as you said," said Monkey.

"But you haven't left my hand – look," said the Buddha. Monkey saw his words written on the middle finger of the Buddha's hand, and there was also the strong smell of monkey urine. At last, Monkey knew that he had met his match.

PERSONALITY

Independent, astute, and sociable, the Monkey can always adapt to new situations. It has an active intellect and loves to rise to a challenge.

Sensitivity is one of your best virtues, and you empathize with the difficulties of others. You are always prepared to fight for a just cause, but are also highly opportunistic, for you suspect that your efforts will enhance your reputation.

MOTIVATION

You have a restless nature and dislike being tied to any situation. You need plenty of activity and variety to stimulate and satisfy your senses. Your keen intellect enables you to assess events quickly and reap the maximum benefit. Although you undoubtedly know how to scheme and manipulate, you use these talents

MONKEY FACE
This impish terra-cotta character hails from the Far East and was made in the 2nd or 3rd century.

wisely, and others can benefit from your astute decisions, as well as yourself. When pushed and cornered by people or events, you react very efficiently. You use your ingenuity to wriggle out of danger, but somehow you never compromise yourself.

THE INNER MONKEY

Your confidence often needs to be boosted, and you can usually be found at the center of a group, entertaining everyone with your excellent sense of humor and inspired argument. You can become too loud and dominant, however, and may sometimes override other people's opinions.

Much of this behavior stems from the overwhelming desire to be accepted and understood by other people. When you sense that you have been excluded, you are deeply hurt and feel rejected. You keep these feelings of insecurity well hidden, however, and in public you will appear to make light of the situation.

You are an extremely generous and entertaining friend. It is a genuine pleasure for you to care for other people and to listen to their anxieties and dilemmas. You always make an effort to understand their problems, but, unintentionally, your mind can sometimes wander, because you are ever stimulated by new ideas and interests.

In emotional affairs you are vivacious and enthusiastic, but your relationship must be lively and entertaining to keep your attention.

You are a very loving parent. You are always ready to share your children's enthusiasms and are prepared to tolerate their mistakes.

SITTING MONKEY

The color of jade can range widely, from white to dark green, depending on the iron content. This white and brown jade hardstone monkey was carved in 19th-century China.

THE MONKEY CHILD

The young Monkey has a lively imagination and is highly adaptable at home or at school. It can easily become overexcited and may need encouragement to calm down. The Monkey child has a tendency to be very critical and could benefit from learning to be more patient.

· MONKEY ·
LOVE

*The Monkey is an alluring creature of immense intelligence
and enthusiasm. Once the Monkey meets its match, it
makes a loving and committed partner.*

At the beginning of a relationship, you are intoxicated with passion and excitement, but as they inevitably fade, you tend to become more critical.

Weaknesses are hard for you to ignore, and once you sense that all is not well in your relationship, you are tempted to run away. You have a charming nature and love to please, but your partner must always be alert and attentive to your needs.

Sometimes your unpredictability can spoil potential happiness. However, when you meet someone you can completely trust, and who can keep you surprised and stimulated, you should be able to enjoy a very successful relationship.

Ideally, you are suited to the Rat and the Dragon. The Rat's wisdom, passion, and opportunism attract you, but it must beware of your moods. You and the Dragon should find each other mutually enchanting, and it will be charmed by your varied skills. The Ox enjoys your vivacity, and

GODDESS OF LOVE
*Kuan Yin is a powerful
figure in Chinese mythology.
Once a male Buddhist deity,
she is now known as the
goddess of mercy, and
as Sung-tzu, the giver
of children.*

Find your animal sign, then look for the animals that share its background color – the Monkey has a pink background and is most compatible with the Rat and the Dragon. The symbol in the center of the wheel represents double happiness.

you should appreciate its stability. If you can manage to curb your criticism, you could be compatible with the adventurous Tiger. Your astute nature appeals to the discreet Rabbit, and it will offer you understanding and tenderness. You relish another Monkey's alert intelligence and audacity, and the honest Pig should be able to understand your many wiles and schemes.

ORCHID

In China, the orchid, or Lan Hua, *is an emblem of love and beauty. It is also a fertility symbol and represents many offspring.*

Relationships with the Ram, Dog, Rooster, Snake, and Horse may be demanding. Your liveliness is shared by the Ram, but it may need too much support, and the Dog could resent your carefree approach. Although you are as sociable as the Rooster, you rarely feel happy with each other. Your unpredictability may distress the Snake, but you can appreciate each other's intelligence. The Horse is extremely dependent on its emotions and may find you too insensitive as a partner.

· MONKEY ·
CAREER

The Monkey is a diligent worker and needs plenty of variety and challenges. It dislikes routine and feels trapped by a predictable career.

Currency

STOCKBROKER

Even when it is under extreme or unexpected pressure, the Monkey always knows how to take the best possible care of its financial or personal interests. Consequently, it can be an extremely successful stockbroker.

Celadon monkey

Bottle of holy water

THEOLOGIAN

A career as a theologian makes use of the Monkey's communication skills, and the academic demands of theology appeal to its sharp intellect. The seated celadon monkey on the right is from 16th- or 17th-century China. As an incense burner, it was used to facilitate religious communication.

ROVING REPORTER

The Monkey has a quick mind, is willing to travel, and is happiest when it has to call upon its ingenuity. All these qualities make the Monkey ideally suited to a journalistic career.

Airplane

Chinese fan

ARTISTIC DESIGNER

Although the Monkey is not overly renowned for its artistic skills, it is nevertheless a gifted creature. It has the potential to pursue an artistic career, perhaps as a calligrapher. The calligraphy on this 19th-century Chinese fan is painted in gold.

Measuring instrument

Maps

PLANNER

The Monkey has an astute, uncanny eye for opportunities and is a good planner. It makes decisions swiftly and correctly when necessary.

HEALTH

Yin and yang are in a continual state of flux within the body. Good health is dependent upon the balance of yin and yang being constantly harmonious.

There is a natural minimum and maximum level of yin and yang in the human body. The body's energy is known as ch'i and is a yang force. The movement of ch'i in the human body is complemented by the movement of blood, which is a yin force. The very slightest displacement of the balance of yin or yang in the human body can quickly lead to poor health and sickness.

LINGCHIH FUNGUS
The fungus shown in this detail from a Ch'ing dynasty bowl is the "immortal" lingchih fungus, which symbolizes longevity.

CHINESE WOLFBERRY
The root bark of this very powerful herb is often used in Chinese medicine to treat diabetic disorders.

However, yang illness can be cured by yin treatment, and yin illness can be cured by yang treatment. Everybody has their own individual balance of yin and yang. It is likely that a hot-tempered person will have strong yang forces, and that a peaceful person will have strong yin forces. Your nature is closely identified with your health, and before prescribing Chinese medicine, your moods have to be carefully taken into account. A balance of joy, anger, sadness, happiness, worry, pensiveness, and fear must always be maintained. This fine balance is known in China as the Harmony of the Seven Sentiments.

Born in the Year of the Monkey, you are associated with the element gold. This element is linked with the lungs, large intestine, nose, skin, and hair. These are the parts of the human body that are most relevant to the pattern of your health. You are also associated with the emotion of sorrow and with acrid-tasting food.

The root bark of Chinese wolfberry (*Lycium chinense*) is associated with your Chinese astrological sign. Its seeds are used in the restoration of the liver and kidneys, and in the treatment of diabetes. The root bark is often added to a Chinese yam soup, which has the reputed ability to strengthen the spleen, stomach, lungs, and kidneys. This soup is also used to treat diabetic thirst.

Chinese medicine is specific; therefore, never take Chinese wolfberry or any other herb unless you are following professional advice from a fully qualified Chinese or Western doctor.

ASTROLOGY AND ANATOMY
Your element, gold, is associated with two major organs, the lungs and the large intestine. The lungs are yin, and the large intestine is yang.

· MONKEY ·
LEISURE

The Monkey is skilled with its hands and loves to make or repair objects. It enjoys variety and is attracted by challenges and interesting people and places.

ROULETTE

Games of chance are enjoyable pastimes for the Monkey, because it loves to gamble. It is a mischievous creature, however, and is likely to be prepared to cheat in order to win.

Roulette wheel

Chinese jade monkey riding a pony

HORSE RACING

In China, the gift of a monkey riding on a pony expresses the wish that the recipient may be promoted soon. However, the Monkey has other connections with horses, usually in the form of a day at the races. The Monkey admires the jockeys' skill and the horses' speed, but most importantly, it likes to gamble on the outcome of the race.

Riding whip

Jester's shoes

ENTERTAINING
The Monkey is a great entertainer, a natural clown, and if it held a place at court, it would undoubtedly be the jester. The Monkey is at its best when faced with the unexpected, because this allows it to rely upon its impish ingenuity.

Running shoe

RUNNING
Although the Monkey dislikes the routine of a heavy training schedule, it enjoys the solitary nature of running, and competition and challenges spur it to ever greater heights.

Beach ball

Water-skiing gloves

WATER SPORTS
The Monkey enjoys all sports that involve speed, but it is particularly attracted to water sports such as waterskiing. It always manages to keep itself amused, even by something as simple as playing with a beach ball.

SYMBOLISM

*Each astrological animal is linked with a certain food,
direction, color, emotion, association, and symbol. The
Monkey is also associated with the season of Autumn.*

Porcelain
monkeys

COLOR
In China, brilliant white is the
color of purity. It is also the
color that is linked with the
Monkey. This group of four
porcelain monkeys is from
China's Ch'ing dynasty.

Cloves

FOOD
Acrid foods, such as cloves, are
associated with the Monkey.

Chinese antique compass

T-square

SYMBOL
The Monkey's symbol in
Chinese astrology is the
T-square.

DIRECTION
The Chinese compass points south,
whereas the Western compass points
north. The Monkey's direction is the west.

EMOTION
Sorrow is the emotion that is
connected with the Monkey.

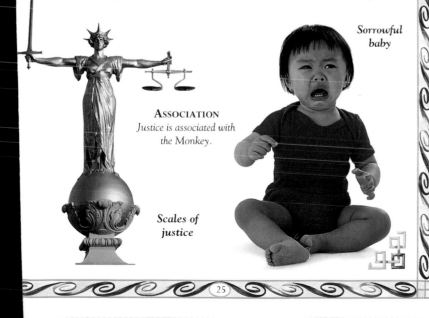

Sorrowful baby

ASSOCIATION
Justice is associated with
the Monkey.

Scales of justice

MONKEY CLIMBING A TREE

~ 1944 2004 ~

*This Monkey is in its natural environment and makes the
most of its opportunity. It is associated with trees and
success, which is a very auspicious combination.*

The Monkey is a lucky sign, but
there are some difficult aspects to its
personality. Luckily, the good
fortune of the Monkey Climbing a
Tree outweighs these aspects.

PERSONALITY

You are likely to be a remarkable
person. This should help you
throughout your life, but may also
produce some frustrations. You
could be accused of arrogance, for
you often feel that if you were only
given the chance, you could be far
more successful than those around
you. As a result, other people may
consider you to be impatient, or
even just plain rude.

You will probably find it very
difficult to work in a group or a
team. Try to be patient, for your
skills and versatility are likely to be
recognized eventually, and you
should realize your full potential.

FRIENDSHIPS

The natural vitality of the Monkey
personality is likely to make you
very popular with your friends.
Once you have tasted the fruits of
success, your friends will probably
be able to enjoy your company even
further, for you will be very much
more relaxed.

RELATIONSHIPS

Try to be calm and patient in your
emotional life, and do not rush into a
long-term commitment. You may
have to wait a long time before you
meet the right person, but when you
eventually find your partner, you
should be able to enjoy an excellent
relationship together.

PARENTHOOD

It is likely that you will not have
children for many years, but this will
invariably prove beneficial. This is

Monkey Climbing a Tree

because once you are firmly established in your career, you will be more capable of giving your family the support and attention that they need and deserve.

PROSPECTS

As you mature, your considerable skills should be appreciated. Consequently, you are likely to be very successful and should lead a comfortable life. Your progress through life should become increasingly smooth, but always beware of the typical Monkey trait of lying when you think it might be useful. This deceitful characteristic could undo all your good luck, and you must therefore aim to keep it always under firm control.

MONKEY CLIMBING UP THE MOUNTAIN

~ 1956 2016 ~

This Monkey enjoys the challenge of climbing up a mountain. However, since it is out of its natural environment, the challenge can become very stressful.

You are associated with the fire in the home. Symbolically, this signifies that you have the capacity to warm and be comforting, but also to burn and be damaging. Consequently, you must exercise care and restraint in all areas of your life.

You have great potential and personal promise, but may also have to encounter and take considerable risks. However, as long as you always try to follow the correct course, you have a very good chance of being successful.

PERSONALITY

Your main problem in life is the tendency to overextend yourself. Most Monkeys firmly believe that they can take on any challenge – even climbing a mountain – and win comfortably, but you must try to take sufficient care of yourself.

Even though you might enjoy exciting challenges, you are not always able to respond to them with ease and success.

Try to accept the limits of your strength, skills, and intellect, and learn to examine new opportunities with a little more caution. If you are sensible, yet still take on the more realistic challenges and opportunities that may come your way, you should be able to be successful.

RELATIONSHIPS

In emotional matters, do not allow the reckless and selfish aspect of the Monkey personality to rule your life.

It is important for you to be very sure about the risks you are willing to take in your relationships with your partners, whether in your emotional life or in your career. Remember that if you are lured by

Monkey Climbing Up the Mountain

conquests or adventures outside these partnerships, you will invariably suffer as a result.

PROSPECTS

Any financial gains should be treated with great care. Do not be tempted to squander your gains, for you may not have another opportunity to develop them.

It might be beneficial to consider the many advantages of investment — be prepared to forgo immediate benefits, and look forward to enjoying the profits later in life.

Other people are likely to respect this sensible behavior, and in your later years you may even enjoy some fame and good fortune.

You are always likely to be a combination of potential and risk — the same skills and energies that can bring you comfort may also prove to be destructive.

As long as you are discerning and wise, you will learn how to derive warmth and comfort from your personality. Alternatively, if you are careless, you may damage yourself, or other people, instead.

LONELY MONKEY

~ 1908   1968 ~

*Despite its forlorn name, the Lonely Monkey is not
necessarily a sad creature, but unfortunately, it is likely to
suffer difficulties in its family relationships.*

You are associated with cutting, and as a consequence, you find it all too easy to "cut" people down to size.

PERSONALITY
Any problems in your life are likely to be related to this fundamental personality weakness. You are prone to saying exactly what you think. Perhaps you should show more consideration, and try not to be so self-absorbed.

You are naturally very intelligent and quick-minded. This exuberance should be restrained, however, for it is unlikely to be helpful in your relationships with your family or your friends.

You are vulnerable to changes of mood. Although these mood changes are alarming for you, other people are likely to find them even more confusing and bewildering. You are always easily affected by people and

by circumstances, and this is something that you must do your best to control.

FAMILY
Unfortunately, you are likely to experience many difficulties with your family. Your relationship with your parents will probably be bearable, but real problems are likely to ensue in the relationship between you and your children. Your siblings, too, might find you awkward and troublesome to cope with.

PROSPECTS
You tend to be very hardworking, and this should bring you various rewards. Financially, these rewards are likely to be good, but not excessive. Luckily, it is in your nature to be careful with your money, and you should therefore always be financially comfortable.

Lonely Monkey

The combination of your innate intelligence, natural diligence, and ability to take on challenges should draw you to the attention of those in authority. They are likely to note your many qualities and will try to further your career.

You must control your sharp tongue, however, for others, particularly those in authority, might find it irritating and aggravating.

Always beware of your association with cutting, for it suggests that any area of your life could be destroyed, or cut off in its prime, by an unthinking action.

As long as you continue to watch this aspect of your personality and try to control your moods, you should find that you enjoy improved relationships with your family and with your colleagues.

MONKEY IN THE FRUIT TREE

~ 1920 1980 ~

This Monkey is surrounded by delicious fruit, and there is nothing to stop it from indulging itself. Still, life is sometimes not quite as perfect as it might seem.

You are associated with two raised hands, which are balancing a bowl. This is sometimes interpreted as representing equal alternatives, or opposite sides of the same coin. It suggests that the motives behind your actions will not necessarily correspond to the way in which you are perceived by other people.

PERSONALITY

Even if you are impeccably well behaved and completely unselfish, other people are unlikely to praise you or to view your actions kindly. Inevitably, this can be rather frustrating, but do not allow it to become embittering.

Remember that essentially you are a happy-go-lucky person and have excellent opportunities for success and good fortune. These opportunities are unlikely to be appreciated by others, but never give in to feelings of contempt or cynicism, for this could prove personally damaging.

You are likely to be very attractive, and people should find you lively and vivacious, but they may harbor jealous feelings. When confronting the jealousy of others, the best course of action is simply to be true to yourself.

FEMALE CHARACTERISTICS

The female Monkey in the Fruit Tree, in particular, may find that she provokes considerable jealousy. This could be from her friends or even from her family – they may feel that all the good looks and good fortune have gone to her.

FRIENDSHIPS

Surprisingly, it is possible that your good fortune and success sometimes make you feel lonely and friendless.

Monkey in the Fruit Tree

Make sure, therefore, that you always pay sufficient attention to your friendships, and do not assume that they will work out for the best by themselves.

PROSPECTS
Although people in authority will rarely praise you, they should eventually start to appreciate your finer points. Opportunities should be created for you, and you are likely to be able to rise within your chosen career, as long as you are willing to take on every challenge that is offered to you.

Since the Monkey in the Fruit Tree is a fortunate creature, you should try to respond positively to every opportunity.

ELEGANT MONKEY

~ 1932 1992 ~

This Monkey has a complex character, and tends to have a very high opinion of itself. Consequently, the Elegant Monkey can sometimes be accused of arrogance.

You are associated with the ability to increase your yield. This indicates very good fortune, for you are capable of making profit through your own endeavors and know instinctively when it is the best time to reap what you have sown.

PERSONALITY

Sometimes you may seem to have conflicting personality traits. You are highly intelligent, and this could lead to an overconfident, swaggering manner, but you are also very kind.

The natural result of this conflicting combination is often rapid swings in mood. You always like to express your natural exuberance, but if you upset someone by your behavior, you tend to become utterly miserable yourself.

These mood swings are invariably distressing for you, so you must try to control them. Perhaps the best

solution is to apply your considerable intelligence to the problem, and temper it with your innate kindness.

It is important for you to accept your naturally complex nature. Self-acceptance can be a very powerful tool, and hopefully, you will eventually be able to recognize how to use your conflicting personality aspects to your best advantage.

You are careful in your financial affairs, but you have a tendency to go too far and could even be accused of stinginess. Beware of this, for it could lead to trouble. Other people might start to feel peculiarly uneasy in your company or could become suspicious of your real intentions.

Remember that although there is absolutely nothing wrong with being frugal with your money, you should not allow this personality trait to develop into extreme, and ultimately alienating, parsimony.

Elegant Monkey

CAREER

Your mercurial personality might lead to personal fame, but you should also beware of the unwanted attention that the limelight will inevitably bring.

RELATIONSHIPS

If you choose your partner carefully, you should be able to have an excellent committed relationship. Once you have made the correct choice, your partner is likely to be very faithful and supportive. Your children will inevitably benefit from your position in life and should always be a credit to you.

PROSPECTS

You have excellent potential. If you can learn to handle your personality with maturity, but also with a sense of challenge and excitement, it is likely that you will achieve great things. Since you are linked with success and fame, you have a much better chance of enjoying it than most other people.

YOUR CHINESE MONTH OF BIRTH

Find the table with your year of birth, and see where your birthday falls. For example, if you were born on August 30, 1956, you were born in Chinese month 7.

1 You enjoy a challenge. Try to listen to other people, and do not rush into romantic entanglements.

2 You stand by your word, but are not a good judge of situations. Take care in emotional matters.

3 You enjoy your life. Try not to be offhand at work because it could cause you to lose your job.

4 You are hardworking and appreciated by others. You have a very strong sense of justice.

5 You would much rather dream than live in the real world. Try to be realistic and use your skills.

6 You are talented and could be very successful. You are prone to mood swings, however.

7 You are honest, hardworking, and elegant. Usually, you swim easily through life's troubles.

8 You are creative, but can have a severe and puritanical attitude. Try to be less judgmental.

9 You are nervous and easily frightened. Learn to overcome your tendency to retreat from life.

10 You prefer to be in control of events. Your considerable energy attracts many people to you.

11 You are extroverted and unusual. You are likely to become more appreciated as you mature.

12 You are conscientious and thoughtful, but you also have a dark side to your personality.

* Some Chinese years contain double months:	
1944: Month 4	1968: Month 7
April 23 – May 21	July 25 – Aug 23
May 22 – June 20	Aug 24 – Sept 21
2004: Month 2	
Feb 20 – March 20	
March 21 – April 18	

1908		
Feb 2 – March 2	1	
March 3 – March 31	2	
April 1 – April 29	3	
April 30 – May 29	4	
May 30 – June 28	5	
June 29 – July 27	6	
July 28 – Aug 26	7	
Aug 27 – Sept 24	8	
Sept 25 – Oct 24	9	
Oct 25 – Nov 23	10	
Nov 24 – Dec 22	11	
Dec 23 – Jan 21 1909	12	

1920		
Feb 20 – March 19	1	
March 20 – April 18	2	
April 19 – May 17	3	
May 18 – June 15	4	
June 16 – July 15	5	
July 16 – Aug 13	6	
Aug 14 – Sept 11	7	
Sept 12 – Oct 11	8	
Oct 12 – Nov 9	9	
Nov 10 – Dec 9	10	
Dec 10 – Jan 8 1921	11	
Jan 9 – Feb 7	12	

1932		
Feb 6 – March 6	1	
March 7 – April 5	2	
April 6 – May 5	3	
May 6 – June 3	4	
June 4 – July 3	5	
July 4 – Aug 1	6	
Aug 2 – Aug 31	7	
Sept 1 – Sept 29	8	
Sept 30 – Oct 28	9	
Oct 29 – Nov 27	10	
Nov 28 – Dec 26	11	
Dec 27 – Jan 25 1933	12	

1944		
Jan 25 – Feb 23	1	
Feb 24 – March 23	2	
March 24 – April 22	3	
See double months box	4	
June 21 – July 19	5	
July 20 – Aug 18	6	
Aug 19 – Sept 16	7	
Sept 17 – Oct 16	8	
Oct 17 – Nov 15	9	
Nov 16 – Dec 14	10	
Dec 15 – Jan 13 1945	11	
Jan 14 – Feb 12	12	

1956		
Feb 12 – March 11	1	
March 12 – April 10	2	
April 11 – May 9	3	
May 10 – June 8	4	
June 9 – July 7	5	
July 8 – Aug 5	6	
Aug 6 – Sept 4	7	
Sept 5 – Oct 3	8	
Oct 4 – Nov 2	9	
Nov 3 – Dec 1	10	
Dec 2 – Dec 31	11	
Jan 1 – Jan 30 1957	12	

1968		
Jan 30 – Feb 27	1	
Feb 28 – March 28	2	
March 29 – April 26	3	
April 27 – May 26	4	
May 27 – June 25	5	
June 26 – July 24	6	
See double months box	7	
Sept 22 – Oct 21	8	
Oct 22 – Nov 19	9	
Nov 20 – Dec 19	10	
Dec 20 – Jan 17 1969	11	
Jan 18 – Feb 16	12	

1980		
Feb 16 – March 16	1	
March 17 – April 14	2	
April 15 – May 13	3	
May 14 – June 12	4	
June 13 – July 11	5	
July 12 – Aug 10	6	
Aug 11 – Sept 8	7	
Sept 9 – Oct 8	8	
Oct 9 – Nov 7	9	
Nov 8 – Dec 6	10	
Dec 7 – Jan 5 1981	11	
Jan 6 – Feb 4	12	

1992		
Feb 4 – March 3	1	
March 4 – April 2	2	
April 3 – May 2	3	
May 3 – May 31	4	
June 1 – June 29	5	
June 30 – July 29	6	
July 30 – Aug 27	7	
Aug 28 – Sept 25	8	
Sept 26 – Oct 25	9	
Oct 26 – Nov 23	10	
Nov 24 – Dec 23	11	
Dec 24 – Jan 22 1993	12	

2004		
Jan 22 – Feb 19	1	
See double months box	2	
April 19 – May 18	3	
May 19 – June 17	4	
June 18 – July 16	5	
July 17 – Aug 15	6	
Aug 16 – Sept 13	7	
Sept 14 – Oct 13	8	
Oct 14 – Nov 11	9	
Nov 12 – Dec 11	10	
Dec 12 – Jan 9 2005	11	
Jan 10 – Feb 8	12	

YOUR CHINESE DAY OF BIRTH

Refer to the previous page to discover the beginning of your Chinese month of birth, then use the chart below to calculate your Chinese day of birth.

If you were born on May 5, 1908, your birthday is in the month starting on April 30. Find 30 on the chart below. Using 30 as the first day, count the days until you reach the date of your birthday. (Remember that not all months contain 31 days.) You were born on day 6 of the Chinese month.

If you were born in a Chinese double month, simply count the days from the first date of the month that contains your birthday.

1	2	3	4	5	6	7
8	9	10	11	12	13	14
15	16	17	18	19	20	21
22	23	24	25	26	27	28
29	30	31				

DAY 1, 10, 19, OR 28
You are trustworthy and set high standards, but tend to rush your projects. Try to be cautious, and do not be too self-obsessed. You may receive unexpected money but must control your spending. You are suited to a career in the public sector or the arts.

DAY 2, 11, 20, OR 29
You are honest and popular. You need peace, but also require lively company. You are prone to outbursts of temper. You tend to enjoy life and make the most of your opportunities. You are suited to a literary or artistic career.

DAY 3, 12, 21, OR 30
You are quick-witted, but may appear to be difficult. As a result, people may be wary of being your friend. You have a disciplined character and fight for the truth. You are suited to careers that have a competitive element.

Day 4, 13, 22, or 31

You are very warmhearted, but also have a reserved attitude, which can sometimes make you appear unapproachable. If you try to be more outgoing and sociable, you should become more popular. You have a calm and patient manner, and are suited to a career as an academic or researcher.

Day 5, 14, or 23

Your fiery, obstinate nature can sometimes make it difficult for you to accept suggestions or opinions from others, and your stubbornness may lead to quarrels or problems. You should be lucky with money and may often use your profits to set up new projects. Your innate intelligence will enable you to cope with a demanding career.

Day 6, 15, or 24

You have an open, stable, and cheerful character, and enjoy an active social life. You are affectionate and emotional, and have a tendency to daydream. This can lead to confusion, and your eagerness to help others may be stifled by your indecision. Although you will never be wealthy, you should always have enough money.

Day 7, 16, or 25

You enjoy a certain amount of excitement in your life, but must learn to become more realistic and disciplined. Although you are a natural performer, you should beware of alienating your friends or colleagues. In your career, the opportunity to travel is more important to you than a good salary or a high standard of living.

Day 8, 17, or 26

You have very good judgment, but should not act too quickly. Your social skills may sometimes be lacking, and you may alienate other people, so try to be more tactful. You will experience poverty, but also wealth. Your calm and determined nature is combined with a free spirit, making you best suited to self-employment.

Day 9, 18, or 27

You are happy, optimistic, and warmhearted. You keep yourself busy and are rarely troubled by trivialities. Occasionally you quarrel unnecessarily with your friends, and it is important for you to learn to control your moods. You are particularly suited to a career as a sole owner or proprietor.

YOUR CHINESE
HOUR OF BIRTH

*In Chinese time, one hour is equal to two Western hours.
Each Chinese double hour is associated with one of the
twelve astrological animals.*

11 P.M. – 1 A.M. RAT HOUR
You are independent and have a hot temper. Try to think before you speak. Your thrifty nature will be useful in business and at home. You are willing to help those who are close to you, and they will return your support.

1 – 3 A.M. OX HOUR
Up to the age of twenty, your life could be difficult, but your fortunes are likely to improve after these troublesome years. In your career, be prepared to take a risk or to leave home during your youth to achieve your goals. You should enjoy a prosperous old age.

3 – 5 A.M. TIGER HOUR
You have a lively and creative nature, which may cause family arguments in your youth. Between the ages of twenty and forty you may

have many problems. Luckily, your fortunes are likely to improve dramatically in your forties.

5 – 7 A.M. RABBIT HOUR
Your parents should be helpful, but your siblings may be your rivals. You may have to move away from home to achieve your full potential at work. Your committed relationship may take time to become settled, but you should get along much better with everyone after middle age.

7 – 9 A.M. DRAGON HOUR
You have a quick-witted, determined, and attractive nature. Your life will be busy, but you could sometimes be lonely. You should achieve a good standard of living. Try to curb your excessive self-confidence, for it could make working relationships difficult.

9 – 11 A.M. SNAKE HOUR
You have a talent for business and should find it easy to build your career and provide for your family. You have a very generous spirit and will gladly help your friends when they are in trouble. Unfortunately, family relationships are unlikely to run smoothly.

11 A.M. – 1 P.M. HORSE HOUR
You are active, clever, and obstinate. Try to listen to advice. You are fascinated with travel and with changing your life. Learn to control your extravagance, for it could lead to financial suffering.

1 – 3 P.M. RAM HOUR
Steady relationships with your family, friends, or partners are difficult, because you have an active nature. You are clever, but must not force your views on others. Your fortunes will be at their lowest in your middle age.

3 – 5 P.M. MONKEY HOUR
You earn and spend money easily. Your character is attractive, but frustrating, too. Sometimes your parents are not able to give you adequate moral support. Your committed relationship should be good, but do not brood over emotional problems for too long – if you do your career could suffer.

5 – 7 P.M. ROOSTER HOUR
In your teenage years you may have many arguments with your family. There could even be a family division, which should eventually be resolved. You are trustworthy, kind, and warmhearted, and never intend to hurt other people.

7 – 9 P.M. DOG HOUR
Your brave, capable, hard-working nature is ideally suited to self-employment, and the forecast for your career is excellent. Try to control your impatience and vanity. The quality of your life is far more important to you than the amount of money you have saved.

9 – 11 P.M. PIG HOUR
You are particularly skilled at manual work and always set yourself high standards. Although you are warmhearted, you do not like to surround yourself with too many friends. However, the people who are close to you have your complete trust. You can be easily upset by others, but are able to forgive and forget quickly.

YOUR FORTUNE IN OTHER ANIMAL YEARS

The Monkey's fortunes fluctuate during the twelve animal years. It is best to concentrate on a year's positive aspects, and to take care when faced with the seemingly negative.

YEAR OF THE RAT
Although you should have success during the Year of the Rat, you are unlikely to enjoy it to the fullest. This is largely because you are haunted by something from your past. Once you have resolved your inner conflict, you should do well.

YEAR OF THE OX
This is a highly auspicious year for your family life and your professional life. You will have to cope with some problems, but they are relatively minor and should not mar the success and happiness of the Year of the Ox in any way.

YEAR OF THE TIGER
You will encounter problems in your home life, which will force you to travel. During your travels you will overcome your financial difficulties. As as result, your family life should become easier.

YEAR OF THE RABBIT
Everything that you decide to try your hand at is a great success in the Year of the Rabbit. Other people might wonder why you should suddenly be blessed with the Midas touch, but your rewards are no more than you deserve.

YEAR OF THE DRAGON
Your fortunes are fairly mixed, and you will feel thoroughly unsettled. However, the Year of the Dragon will also bring you success in unlikely ways. You are susceptible to accidents this year; therefore, take care, and think before you act.

YEAR OF THE SNAKE

Although you will enjoy the favor of people in authority during the Year of the Snake, you will still seem to have more than your fair share of troubles. The root cause of these problems is most likely to be other people's resentment.

YEAR OF THE HORSE

A seemingly never-ending variety of trials and tribulations are likely to pursue you throughout this difficult year. Keep calm, and remember that as long as you are thoughtful and cautious, some of these difficulties can be avoided.

YEAR OF THE RAM

Unfortunately, this is not one of the best years for the Monkey. You are particularly susceptible to poor health. Illness will debilitate you and make you feel frustrated and lonely; therefore, make a determined effort to look after yourself.

YEAR OF THE MONKEY

This is your own year, and you expect to have good fortune. You will not be disappointed and should make a full recovery from last year's depression. Friendships will be very rewarding, and you should make an effort to rebuild them.

YEAR OF THE ROOSTER

You must be very careful in all areas of your life, because it is likely that you will find the year extremely tough and demanding. Try to be on your best behavior, and choose your friends and acquaintances with care.

YEAR OF THE DOG

Your behavior could cause considerable distress during the Year of the Dog. You may be personally affected by this distress, or it could affect other people instead. In any case, this year is likely to be difficult, tiring, and perplexing.

YEAR OF THE PIG

This is a year in which you need to exercise great care and restraint in all of your financial affairs. You may be tempted to travel excessively. Try to resist, for the costs could be very high in emotional as well as financial terms.

YOUR CHINESE YEAR OF BIRTH

Your astrological animal corresponds to the Chinese year of your birth. It is the single most important key in the quest to unlock your Chinese horoscope.

Find your Western year of birth in the left-hand column of the chart. Your Chinese astrological animal is on the same line as your year of birth in the right-hand column of the chart. If you were born in the beginning of the year, check the middle column of the chart carefully. For example, if you were born in 1969, you might assume that you belong to the Year of the Rooster. However, if your birthday falls before February 17, you actually belong to the Year of the Monkey.

1900	Jan 31 – Feb 18, 1901	Rat
1901	Feb 19 – Feb 7, 1902	Ox
1902	Feb 8 – Jan 28, 1903	Tiger
1903	Jan 29 – Feb 15, 1904	Rabbit
1904	Feb 16 – Feb 3, 1905	Dragon
1905	Feb 4 – Jan 24, 1906	Snake
1906	Jan 25 – Feb 12, 1907	Horse
1907	Feb 13 – Feb 1, 1908	Ram
1908	Feb 2 – Jan 21, 1909	Monkey
1909	Jan 22 – Feb 9, 1910	Rooster
1910	Feb 10 – Jan 29, 1911	Dog
1911	Jan 30 – Feb 17, 1912	Pig
1912	Feb 18 – Feb 5, 1913	Rat
1913	Feb 6 – Jan 25, 1914	Ox
1914	Jan 26 – Feb 13, 1915	Tiger
1915	Feb 14 – Feb 2, 1916	Rabbit
1916	Feb 3 – Jan 22, 1917	Dragon

1917	Jan 23 – Feb 10, 1918	Snake
1918	Feb 11 – Jan 31, 1919	Horse
1919	Feb 1 – Feb 19, 1920	Ram
1920	Feb 20 – Feb 7, 1921	Monkey
1921	Feb 8 – Jan 27, 1922	Rooster
1922	Jan 28 – Feb 15, 1923	Dog
1923	Feb 16 – Feb 4, 1924	Pig
1924	Feb 5 – Jan 23, 1925	Rat
1925	Jan 24 – Feb 12, 1926	Ox
1926	Feb 13 – Feb 1, 1927	Tiger
1927	Feb 2 – Jan 22, 1928	Rabbit
1928	Jan 23 – Feb 9, 1929	Dragon
1929	Feb 10 – Jan 29, 1930	Snake
1930	Jan 30 – Feb 16, 1931	Horse
1931	Feb 17 – Feb 5, 1932	Ram
1932	Feb 6 – Jan 25, 1933	Monkey
1933	Jan 26 – Feb 13, 1934	Rooster

Year	Dates	Animal		Year	Dates	Animal
1934	Feb 14 – Feb 3, 1935	Dog		1971	Jan 27 – Feb 14, 1972	Pig
1935	Feb 4 – Jan 23, 1936	Pig		1972	Feb 15 – Feb 2, 1973	Rat
1936	Jan 24 – Feb 10, 1937	Rat		1973	Feb 3 – Jan 22, 1974	Ox
1937	Feb 11 – Jan 30, 1938	Ox		1974	Jan 23 – Feb 10, 1975	Tiger
1938	Jan 31 – Feb 18, 1939	Tiger		1975	Feb 11 – Jan 30, 1976	Rabbit
1939	Feb 19 – Feb 7, 1940	Rabbit		1976	Jan 31 – Feb 17, 1977	Dragon
1940	Feb 8 – Jan 26, 1941	Dragon		1977	Feb 18 – Feb 6, 1978	Snake
1941	Jan 27 – Feb 14, 1942	Snake		1978	Feb 7 – Jan 27, 1979	Horse
1942	Feb 15 – Feb 4, 1943	Horse		1979	Jan 28 – Feb 15, 1980	Ram
1943	Feb 5 – Jan 24, 1944	Ram		1980	Feb 16 – Feb 4, 1981	Monkey
1944	Jan 25 – Feb 12, 1945	Monkey		1981	Feb 5 – Jan 24, 1982	Rooster
1945	Feb 13 – Feb 1, 1946	Rooster		1982	Jan 25 – Feb 12, 1983	Dog
1946	Feb 2 – Jan 21, 1947	Dog		1983	Feb 13 – Feb 1, 1984	Pig
1947	Jan 22 – Feb 9, 1948	Pig		1984	Feb 2 – Feb 19, 1985	Rat
1948	Feb 10 – Jan 28, 1949	Rat		1985	Feb 20 – Feb 8, 1986	Ox
1949	Jan 29 – Feb 16, 1950	Ox		1986	Feb 9 – Jan 28, 1987	Tiger
1950	Feb 17 – Feb 5, 1951	Tiger		1987	Jan 29 – Feb 16, 1988	Rabbit
1951	Feb 6 – Jan 26, 1952	Rabbit		1988	Feb 17 – Feb 5, 1989	Dragon
1952	Jan 27 – Feb 13, 1953	Dragon		1989	Feb 6 – Jan 26, 1990	Snake
1953	Feb 14 – Feb 2, 1954	Snake		1990	Jan 27 – Feb 14, 1991	Horse
1954	Feb 3 – Jan 23, 1955	Horse		1991	Feb 15 – Feb 3, 1992	Ram
1955	Jan 24 – Feb 11, 1956	Ram		1992	Feb 4 – Jan 22, 1993	Monkey
1956	Feb 12 – Jan 30, 1957	Monkey		1993	Jan 23 – Feb 9, 1994	Rooster
1957	Jan 31 – Feb 17, 1958	Rooster		1994	Feb 10 – Jan 30, 1995	Dog
1958	Feb 18 – Feb 7, 1959	Dog		1995	Jan 31 – Feb 18, 1996	Pig
1959	Feb 8 – Jan 27, 1960	Pig		1996	Feb 19 – Feb 6, 1997	Rat
1960	Jan 28 – Feb 14, 1961	Rat		1997	Feb 7 – Jan 27, 1998	Ox
1961	Feb 15 – Feb 4, 1962	Ox		1998	Jan 28 – Feb 15, 1999	Tiger
1962	Feb 5 – Jan 24, 1963	Tiger		1999	Feb 16 – Feb 4, 2000	Rabbit
1963	Jan 25 – Feb 12, 1964	Rabbit		2000	Feb 5 – Jan 23, 2001	Dragon
1964	Feb 13 – Feb 1, 1965	Dragon		2001	Jan 24 – Feb 11, 2002	Snake
1965	Feb 2 – Jan 20, 1966	Snake		2002	Feb 12 – Jan 31, 2003	Horse
1966	Jan 21 – Feb 8, 1967	Horse		2003	Feb 1 – Jan 21, 2004	Ram
1967	Feb 9 – Jan 29, 1968	Ram		2004	Jan 22 – Feb 8, 2005	Monkey
1968	Jan 30 – Feb 16, 1969	Monkey		2005	Feb 9 – Jan 28, 2006	Rooster
1969	Feb 17 – Feb 5, 1970	Rooster		2006	Jan 29 – Feb 17, 2007	Dog
1970	Feb 6 – Jan 26, 1971	Dog		2007	Feb 18 – Feb 6, 2008	Pig